Great British Running Routes

The Ultimate Guide of the Best Trails in the UK You Need to Complete

Charles Goodwill

Table of Contents

Introduction

Congratulations on purchasing *Great British Running Routes: The Ultimate Guide of The Best Trails in the UK You Need to Complete,* and thank you for doing so.

In this book, you will discover some of the most amazing areas of the UK that have fantastic running routes and picturesque scenery. We will go over 70 different places where you can find some of the best runnings, or walking, routes in the UK. They vary in difficulty, and some of them take multiple days to complete.

Thank you for choosing this book, and I hope you find it helpful.

Chapter 1: The Rye Ancient Trail

Located in East Sussex, United Kingdom, The Rye Ancient Trail offers an all-terrain running track which is considered as one of the best by the local athletes. It's a fantastic route accompanied by some magnificent views, steep climbing zones, pastoral orchards, vineyards, and some country lanes. The races are of 15km or 30km route, accompanied by 1500 ft. of climbing, which is estimated to be a good start for newcomers and seasoned runners. To avoid risk and hazards, we should always get a good grip of the terrain and be careful while running or hiking. This trail was designed and started by top athletes of the time, Jeff Pyrah and Sam Murphy. This challenging route winds its way through footpaths, country lanes, farmlands, and whatnot. It links Iden, Northiam, Beckley to Norman churches of Rye, making it a perfect steeplechase for the runners. The route encompasses several villages, which have their respective traditions, food habits, and conduct of living. These local villages offer you a home close to nature for your ideal vacation stay away from the city lights.

The race starts on the High Street of The George in Rye, followed by a short climb past St. Mary's Church and the ancient Citadel. The course then leads to Domesday (a village of Iden), where local foods like jaffa cakes and jellies are abundant. The 15km and 30 km routes split in Peasmarsh. A number of nearly 400 athletes join this multi-terrain race making it one of the most popular trails in the local area. This race starts and ends in the same medieval town of Rye. The mesmerizing scenic beauty keeps one on their toes and motivated to finish the route no matter how tiresome it becomes for the runners. The bountiful harvests and greenery all the way around make it a pleasure to the eyes to witness this heavenly climb. It is an all-time recommendation for runners, walkers, cyclers, and hikers.

Chapter 2: North Downs Way National Trail

This national trail of 246km is located in South-Eastern England, UK. The route runs from Farnham to Dover along Kent Downs and the Surrey Hills, considered an "Area of outstanding natural beauty (AONB)." The pathway is a mixed-terrain, including footpaths, ridges, country roads, and some undulating slopes. In most parts of the trail, the soil is chalky, and the grassland is mostly calcareous due to the underlying sedimentary chalk deposit. One should be careful about their steps to avoid undesirable mishaps. The elevation of the highest point is approximately 885ft (270 m). Other than the age-old popular Pilgrim's Way, this North Downs Way Trail is considered one of the best in the local area. This trail can be visited at any time of the year during any season.

The race conducted here is recognized as the second race in a 50-mile grand slam. In the run, Box Hill is the steepest climb for the runners. There are few qualifications or rather eligibility tests for the runners in order to participate in the race. Anthony Greenwood, then Minister of Housing and Local Government, was the first to start this trial on 14th July 1969. At the time of opening, the trail was 227km long, which was later extended to 246km in the later years. The route was chosen and designed to provide the walker, runner, or cyclist the best scenic views. The specialty of this national pathway is that it passes through various Napoleonic forts and Neolithic sites, which are exclusive heritage sites of national importance. An abundant reserve of wildlife can be witnessed here, along with surplus varieties of flora and fauna. The trail is also home to some extraordinary artworks like the Will Nash in Guildford, Tunnard at Dorking, and several others in Surrey. Therefore, this national trail is significant in terms of picturesque beauty, topographical variations, and brilliant artworks.

Chapter 3: South Downs Way National Trail

This trail, being one of the well-known national trails of England, attracts thousands of visitors every year. This is primarily for its unparalleled scenic beauty and far-sighted views, and proximity to the endless blue sky. The trail starts from Winchester, Hampshire, and leads all the way to end in Eastbourne of East Sussex. The 160Km long route makes a perfect trail to get away from all the city din. The trail is full of ancient sites, forts, and historical burial sites. Beautiful rivers like Ouse, Meon, and Cuckmere are found flowing amidst various pathways during the trail. Unique historical sites, abundant rivers in between mainly contribute to its popularity.

It is a 100-mile running race with around 500 runners as participants every year. There is an eligibility test for runners to participate. There is an adequate medical support and 13 aid stations to help the runners in case of a physical emergency. The South Downs Way was officially recognized as a national trial in 1963 and opened in 1972. It is considered an easy trail with a maximum elevation of 890 ft (270 m) at Butser Hill. If you are on the trail simply for enjoying a leisurely time or for some fitness training, you can solve both purposes in the best possible way. The trail is suitable for the whole year but is at its best during the spring and autumn season. A decent amount of accommodation and abundant restaurants at reasonable rates are present throughout the pathway, and also a number of villages whose local foods are an absolute delicacy and should not be missed at any cost. This trail is regarded as one of the most beautiful tracks of England, exclusively for the undulating terrain, abundant eateries, best scenic views, and its picture post-card beauty throughout. It's an absolutely recommended place to visit for an ideal getaway from the busy schedule.

Chapter 4: The Ridgeway National Trail

The trail is recognized as a national one and is one of the oldest routes, which runs in remote parts of Southern England, United Kingdom. This route of 139 Km is appropriate for day hiking, walks, camping, cycling, or a quick getaway from work and can be visited during any season of the year. The pathway starts from Overton Hill, near Avebury, and ends in Ivinghoe Beacon, Buckinghamshire. This is located close to Silbury Hill, which is the largest man-made hill on the continent. Local people have been using this route for 5000 years approximately. In medieval times, the pathway was used by people to move their animals carrying goods to the city markets. But the trial was designated officially in the year 1972 by the then Government and was started in 1973. Trails like these are always a good option to spend your holiday.

A 86 mile running race along the Ridgeway is held every year. It is arranged under the supervision of the Trail Running Association. The terrain varies from green lanes to sections of metalled roads and chalky paths as well. It is a bridleway and hence a perfect place for horse riders as well. The trail passes through many Neolithic sites of the Iron Age and Bronze Age, covering Segsbury Castle, Barbury Castle, Avebury Stone Circle, etc. Other than these historical sites, the Ridgeway also passes through a number of beautiful locations like Marlborough, Wanborough, Swindon, Thames, West & East Isley, etc. Several times in recent history, The Ridgeway National Trail has been featured as one of the prime wonders of the South. A number of picturesque villages with very few settlements are a part of the route, making it more attractive. On a concluding note, this trail is one of the most recommended in that area, be it for the best scenic views, easy terrain, exclusive historical sites, or the associated villages nearby.

Chapter 5: Wemyss Bay, Firth of Clyde

In the Central Lowlands of Scotland lies a small village named Wemyss Bay, on the Firth of Clyde. It is a starting point or rather the port for ferries taking passengers to Rothesay. The village was initially a part of the Kelly Estate, which was later transformed into the Kelly Castle. Located 8 miles from Greenock and approximately 32 miles from Glasgow, the village takes advantage of its good locus. The humidity is considerably high here owing to surrounding water bodies. A person named Charles Wilson Brown contributed a lot to the gradual development of the Bay. He took the initiative to build castles, designing new structures so that the city of Wemyss Bay could rise further in aspects of heritage, culture, and subsequent developments in all fields. Several churches were also built during that period by various influential people of those times.

The village was named after an 18th-century inhabitant of the Bay and a fisherman by profession, Robert Wemyss. The Wemyss Bay Station is significantly popular for its historical importance. Some minor caves and few red sandstone structures are also found in this Bay. The Bay has gentle slopes at times and rocky terrain at certain instants, making it a mixed terrain with varying topography. An important thing to keep in mind is that we should get a good grip to avoid unwanted hazards during the trial. Regarded as one of the finest stations in the United Kingdom, all credits to the brilliantly carved Iron structures and glasswork. The station was renovated and rebuilt in 1903 by James Miller, a popular architect, and Donald Mathieson, a known engineer of those times. If you are looking for a relaxing getaway from home, this is the place you are looking for.

Chapter 6: South West Coast Path National Trail

This trail is England's longest one and runs for about 1014 Km (630 miles). It is one of the most challenging routes because of its frequent rise and fall at every river mouth. The elevation of the trail has been found to be almost four times the elevation of Mount Everest. The trail is suitable for all seasons throughout the year. Despite the mesmerizing beauty and the pleasant surroundings, one should be extremely careful about the cliff paths and while crossing rivers. The pathway starts in Somerset at Minehead and ends in Dorset at Poole Harbour. Due to its extremely long route, it is avoided by people at times owing to various factors.

This route takes one through several national parks and heritage sites that add to the attractiveness of the trail. East Devon Coast and Dorset are the two World Heritage sites that come under this trail. The trial was started in 1978. Being the longest route of England and hence covering inevitably a large area, intersects or connects to a large number of other routes at various places. Thousands of visitors visit the place every year throughout all seasons. With breathtaking coastal beauty, lush, filled countryside roads, and rivers every now and then, it is extremely suitable for hiking, walking, and running purposes.

Chapter 7: Pennine Way National Trail

This national trail extends from Edale of Derbyshire district and ends at Kirk Yetholm. The stretch is about 431 Km (268 miles), and the highest point of elevation is about 2930 ft (893 m). The trail runs along the hills of Pennine, which is regarded as England's backbone. Although suitable throughout all seasons of the year, the trail is not absolutely an easy one. One of the prime hazards of this route is the severe weather conditions, liable to changes anytime and every time with zero predictability. It is said to be a little strenuous compared to the other local trails of the area and also believed by some to be England's toughest trail. One should be absolutely careful with their steps in order to avoid the chances of mishap.

The trail was started in the year of 1965 after the route was checked and certified by the British Army. The pathway is intersected by numerous roads and passes and also encompasses several villages, towns linked by adequate means and modes of transport. But, owing to such a huge number of visitors every year, there has been considerable erosion of the terrain and other damages which need attention. One unique and noteworthy fact about this national trail is that it has attracted innumerable writers, some of them being Simon Armitage, Stephenson, Mark Wallington, etc.

Chapter 8: Coffin Route, Ambleside

This route is basically an easy walk between Ambleside and Grasmere. It is an ancient road that was used in medieval times to carry the dead and decayed to the St. Oswald's Church for burial purposes. Rydal Water is present in the pathway, about which we had extensively known for Wordsworth's death here in 1850. A lot of superstitions were associated with this place. In the earlier days, spirits and corpses were feared, linking them with something paranormal. Hence the path was avoided by people in medieval times. Nonetheless, with progressing times and literacy amongst people, these superstitions were washed away from their minds. It is regarded as an easy walk and has sufficient transportation services around the place. There are plenty of local Herdwick sheep to keep you entertained and also a company throughout. One more attraction of the Rydal is its St. Mary's Church, built by Lady le Fleming with the help of Wordsworth in the year 1824.

One of the main attractions here is the Dove Cottage, where Wordsworth used to stay along with his sister for few years. He penned down some of his best works while staying here, and hence anyone who would want to know the poet better must visit the place. There are some beautiful open gardens, a community vegetable garden and some museums, brilliant exhibitions that add to the attraction of the place. The pathway can be a little muddy due to abundant lakes and rivers or a little uneven at few places. Usually, the trail takes around 3-4 hours to complete. The summers are a little crowded usually but the winter months are solemn and empty. Winter is the right time for those who look for a calm and composed place to go for. One short climb and a fairly easy terrain will give you a perfect journey and a pleasant experience.

Chapter 9: Hadrian's Wall

This wall runs from Wallsend in the east to Bowess-on-Solway in the west, stretching for about 1480 m (73 miles), and is the largest archeological Roman structure of Great Britain. The Hadrian's Wall was said to be the epitome of strength, determination, and resourcefulness of the whole empire. It indicated the firmness and well-being of countrymen. The walk along this archeological feature is a magnificent one offering the visitors some of the best sceneries of the UK. The weather here is a little dry but mostly suitable for everyone.

This wall has a history and a strong purpose of construction. In the long-lost history, when Hadrian had gained access to the throne of Britain, there was political unrest and rebellion all over. Emperors of various kingdoms were on the verge of conquering places, and hence there was a troublesome atmosphere. Hence Hadrian got this wall constructed to give protection to his kingdom from the intruders. It became a physical barrier for the enemies and also gave the Roman province an observation point to predict incoming attacks beforehand. Not only for defense purposes, the wall indirectly brought help to a large number of people. This is because thousands of soldiers and common men have been employed in the construction as well as maintenance of this vast structure. One specialty of the wall is that it has a shiny surface that reflects sunlight making it visible for miles. Apart from the run, the exclusively minute details of the heritage sites you get to witness will make you feel enriched and enlightened. More than being an attraction, this wall somehow portrays a historical insight of ancient times, and one should not miss out on this experience.

Chapter 10: Along the Regent's Canal

This 13.8 Km long canal across Central London was built in 1820 by James Morgan. It creates a link between the Grand Union Canal and the Thames River of East London. The weather is pleasant here throughout the year. In the year 2012, a Folk Opera was written to celebrate the 200th year of digging the canal, and the musical was run in several parts of London successfully.

Running along this canal is considered as one of the classic runs through the heart of the city, London. A running race of 16 miles is held starting from Seymour Centre and ending at Limehouse Basin. But in the race, the participants have to come back to the Seymour Centre following the same path. The canal was named after Prince Regent, a royal prince of prehistoric times. Reagents Canal was initially used for transferring cargoes. The Regent's Canal serves as a calm and composed conduit for runners, walkers, cyclers, boaters, considering its attractions range from the London Zoo to a floating bookstore and some boat side gardens. Kayak tours are also very prevalent in the canal. The canal also passes through Maida Hills and Lisson Grove Tunnels. Abundant cafes, restaurants, and Regency-style houses by the water edge make it a perfect outing place. As soon as you get off the canal in Paddington, you will witness an extraordinary Rolling Bridge. This bridge curls up into an octagonal structure, which is spectacular to watch. On a concluding note, running at the Regent's Canal or strolling along the sides of the canal can give you the absolute relaxation which you crave after a long week's hustles.

Chapter 11: Tintern Abbey

This 8-kilometer long-running trail starts along the River Wye banks to the vantage point, located at the picturesque border between Wales and England. If you are looking to reinvigorate your soul by being a bit closer to Mother Nature, this spectacular trail complete with lush greenery will provide you with the best of fresh air, a much needed quiet from the bustling city sounds as well as a stunning view of the historical Tintern Abbey ruins and the river Wye once you reach the top of the trail. The view is especially spectacular since Wye serves as the border between England and Wales, which can be seen in full glory at the top of the trail. While the run can be a bit daunting in challenging weather, the entire trail is signposted to minimize any risk of getting lost. The trail is also an excellent spot for bird-watching expeditions or botanical trips, owing to its ecological diversity. There is also a separate 13-kilometer long-running trail that is for the most part off-road and goes through Offas Dyke, the old railway line, and Quarry edge.

If the natural beauty of the place is still not enough to sweep you off your feet, the historian inside you can quench their thirst by visiting the Abbey, which was built almost a millennium ago, in the year 1131 by the Cistercian order. The Abbey is mostly a ruin, following the event of the "Dissolution of Monasteries" in the 16th century, and has considerable archaeological and historical importance.

Chapter 12: Cotswold Way National Trail

If you are an ecologist who is delighted by ecological diversity or a simple person who just wants to be one with Mother Nature, the Cotswold National Trail is sure to sweep you off your feet. The trail, which celebrated its 50th anniversary in the year 2020, extends from Chipping Camden to the city of Bath, a whopping 165 kilometers through some of the most beautiful and iconic English villages complete with lush pastures and woodlands. The entire trail takes about days to complete, during which you will explore the stunning natural beauty, come across 35 different varieties of lavender, pass Neolithic structures such as burial barrows and ancient battle sites. Most notably, the Cotswold escarpment provides a magnificent view of Malvern Hills and the longest river in Great Britain, and the most voluminous one in all of England, the Severn. Running routes are available in a segmented fashion throughout the trail and can be run in 3 to 5 days.

The trail includes some sharp elevation changes, which can be easily traversed by any fit individual. Additionally, the trail is well waymarked, although guidebooks and maps might be useful for exploring all the villages along the trail.

Embarking on the running trail will take you through some of the most iconic villages in England and breathtaking heritage sites and historical places, including but not limited to the burial chambers constructed by the Neanderthals almost 6000 years ago ruins of which are at Belas Knap along the trail. Cotswold National Landscape, the body that maintains the Cotswold National Trail, also comes up with occasional events along with different parts of the trail, which can be checked out at their website. The trail ends at Bath, the Romans built this city to be a spa and is now a bustling city full of "neoclassical Palladian buildings" that blend in wonderfully with the architecture of the ancient baths. While not traveling through the villages, you can explore the natural beauty of the meadows and woodlands and camp out for a night under a clear sky to indulge in some amateur astrophotography.

Chapter 13: Beachy Head, Sussex

If you love heights, the sea, and a stunning view, you should take a run along the chalk headland of East Sussex, Beachy Head. Although the beach is somewhat unorthodox, the name speaks for itself, owing to it being a chalk cliff instead of your regular sandy beaches rising 162 meters above sea level, providing a spectacular view of the English Channel. Beachy Head owes its spectacular geometry to the gradual corrosive action of the waves of the English Channel, which cut the chalk into a series of cliffs dispersed all along the coast of Sussex. The atmosphere is peaceful and romantic, complemented by the presence of the Beachy Head Lighthouse, which improves the aesthetic pleasure for a person taking in the view on a bright sunny morning.

Beachy Head might also appeal to the cinephile in you since the cliff has been used in numerous high-quality productions, including but not limited to The Living Daylight, the 1987 James Bond film where Bond parachutes out of a Rover which overshoots the cliff. It was also featured in "Harry Potter and the Goblet of Fire" which is the fourth movie in the Harry Potter franchise, as the hosting ground for the Quidditch World Cup.

A great route for taking an early morning run, notable running routes include a circular trail going through Eastbourne and Beachy Head. This 8-kilometer long run is sure to reinvigorate your senses as you brisk along the edge of the cliff overlooking the water and enjoying the cool morning breeze while also catering to your sweet tooth as the place has numerous ice cream vans and restaurants, which will serve you with the much-needed delicacies you deserve after your run. Brisk and efficient bus services are available to make sure that even if you are winded up, you have ample means of availing yourself of public transport.

Chapter 14: Loughrigg Fell, Lake District

If your idea of fun is to spend half a day traveling through gorgeous woodlands, traversing through fells while taking in spectacular views of the entire landscape, the Loughrigg Fell in the Lake District should be there pretty high on your to-do list. It is one of the easier trails, great for beginners who want to have a taste of running on elevated terrains without the steep climbing or scrambling involved. Clocking in at around 10 kilometers, this run will take you through the spectacular views of the Lake District and bring you back to the towns of Ambleside or Grasmere.

The walk has some short steep sections followed by an open countryside where nature's beauty is in full glory with undulating hills and the fells surrounded by quite a lot of open waters. Trekking to one of the vantage points offers a beautiful view of Windermere at the false summit. Don't be satisfied with these views as there are truly breathtaking ones at the top! The run-up to the real summit rewards you with views of Grasmere and the fell of Helm Crag behind it. The summit can be very windy, more than you would anticipate while going upwards.

Running back from the summit, you will come across some spectacular caves that are caused by quarrying activities in the region. While they penetrate quite deep into the hillsides, they are often filled with water and notably enhance the charm of the landscape. As you conclude your walk in the town center of Ambleside, a variety of cafes and restaurants are available for a much-needed brunch.

Chapter 15: Noss Mayo and Newton Ferrers, Devon

If your idea of peace is a stroll along the picturesque trails covering English villages, a walk from Noss Mayo, located close to the Southern banks of Newton Creek, to the village of Newton Ferrers, situated on the creeks of one of Yealm's estuaries, is sure to drop your blood pressure to acceptable levels. Your run, which will take place inside the South Devon Area of Outstanding Natural Beauty, will offer stunning views and take you through peaceful landscapes. Starting at Noss Mayo, your running path takes you above the Southern bank of Newton Creek. A fresh breeze of coastal walking takes you to the junction of Newton Creek and the River Yealm estuary. Picturesque cottage areas open into woodlands. You can also take a short detour to enjoy the scenic beauty at Cellar Beach, which provides a magnificent view of the River Yealm and Estuary.

Moving forward, your run will take you through a different woodland, the Brakehill Plantation, crossing which you will come across the open coastline, several meters above sea level, providing sensational views all across Wembury Bay.

Alternatively, starting from Noss Mayo, you could go to Warren Point and take a ferry across the water, which will lead to a steep climb that rewards you with a spectacular view above Wembury Bay. A brisk descent from the high coastline will bring you to Wembury Beach, where you have public restrooms, cafes, and the Wembury Marine Center. Walking along the Wembury beach, the path continues along Langdon Beach and Wembury Point Beach, following which it climbs and arcs towards Bovisand Beach, where you are greeted with amazing views of Plymouth Sound and Plymouth Breakwater. A perfect run for a quiet day of solitude in the English countryside.

Chapter 16: Pen-y-Ghent, Yorkshire Dales

If you are in the mood to embark on a delightful 16-kilometer long-running trek along a National Trail that will test your endurance and reward you with stunning scenic beauty, the trek to Pen-y-Ghent is all you need. The Yorkshire Three Peaks Challenge's Pen-y-Ghent will be the shortest of them, yet it is the best. This magnificent fell entices you to reach its towering summit right from the outset. Halfway up, you will find the amazing sunken cave known as Hull Pot. It is one of England's largest natural holes with a stunning waterfall in wet weather – comes into view. As hard as it might be to believe, this area was once frequented by elephants! Geologically, Pen-y-Ghent has several interesting features, such as an extensive cave system formed from the corrosive action of flowing water over millennia.

Once at the dramatic summit, the last two big peaks, Ingleborough and Whernside, are easily seen in the magnificent views of the Dales. Water flowing east into the River Skirfare and on to the Humber Estuary passes through the peak, while the water flowing west flows into the River Ribble and eventually into the Irish Sea.

Accommodations and restaurants are available plentiful in the lower altitudes of the trail to keep you warm and well-fed before and after your expedition, which is sure to leave a lasting mark in your memory.

Chapter 17: Frensham Common, Surrey Hills

If you fancy an endurance run, or just an active day out with your favorite canine, allow the 8-kilometer long trail located near Farnham in Surrey to make your day a good one. The looped trail covers the two Frensham lakes, the Frensham Great Pond and the Frensham Little Pond, and is an all-year-round accessible trail with small sections on the road and the majority of it in the hands of nature. Historically, the lakes were constructed in the middle ages to cater to the demand for fish that the Bishop of Winchester's Estate placed. A more recent and interesting piece of historical trivia is that Frensham Common was used as a training ground for military tanks during the Second World War. It was during this time that the ponds were drained to not make the area conspicuous to German Bombers!

If you are a cinephile, yet another interesting trivia about the place is that the lakes were used in multiple movies, most notably the 1959 Sherlock Holmes film, "The Hound of Baskervilles" and the 1999 film "The Mummy" where the lakes were used to portray the Nile River.

The trail starts at the Great Pond visitor center and loops back. Along the run, you will come across beach areas and walkways far removed from the main roads, providing peace. Several species of animals, such as the sand lizard and the smooth snake, are also native to this place. Ornithology enthusiasts will also be raptured by the Woodlark, Dartford warbler, and nightjar. The trail is supplemented by Cafes and toilets at the two lakes. Apart from taking a run, yachting is also available on the Great Lake, while accommodations are available in several cottages in the area if you are in the mood for a weekend getaway.

Chapter 18: Loch an Eilein, Cairngorms

If thinking about trekking brings forth forest trails and clear bodies of water to your mind, go for a highland run at Loch an Eilein in the Cairngorms. Loch an Eilein is a stunning body of water that reflects the majestic pines abundant in the Rothiemurchus Forest and a ruined island castle, constructed originally as a place of refuge from thieves and dacoits, add the finishing touch to make this one of Scotland's most popular short runs. The castle has a long history of conflict, which the historians might find interesting while taking a stroll along the beautiful trail, and since the 18th century, the castle has fallen out of use. It was featured in the BBC TV's "Monarch of the Glen" as the site of an island graveyard. The path is outlined with an extra extension around Loch Gamhna, while another option is to ascend Ord Ban for spectacular vistas. Numerous birds such as the spotted flycatcher, the tree pipit, and the whinchat, among others, make this trail a delight for birdwatchers. The setting is ideal for a short running trip or some muddy mountain biking.

The running trail is supplemented with numerous facilities to enhance your experience as a tourist, most of which are located at the Loch an Eilein Park, comprising a visitors center, washrooms, and a car park, which makes it very convenient if you are driving to this place. The trail loops around the loch and is fairly even and clocks at 5 kilometers, thus being highly accessible and suitable for beginner runners as well as enthusiasts and nature lovers.

Chapter 19: Coed-y-Brenin, Snowdonia

Mountain biking or hiking through lush vegetation in a forest is a captivating dream indeed, and what better way for you to realize it at the Coed-y-Brenin located in North Wales in the Snowdonia National Park. Appropriate named the "King's Forest," Coed-y-Brenin's forest trail has a challenging mountain bike trail, initially carved out from rocky terrain. A particularly helpful visitor's center oversees all activities and offers eight mountain biking trails, eight walking trails, and five running trails, all of which are waymarked.

Coed y Brenin's running trails, which are marked, are great for beginners and the more experienced runner. They range in length from one mile to a more challenging 13.5 mile "half marathon."

The running trails comprise the Sarn Helen Trails that take you to the Cefndeuddwr ridge and then bring you down into the Afon Gain valley. The route will take you upstream, along the river until you get to the Penmaen Farm ruins, and then carves up to Sarn Helen before returning to the visitor center. The Half Marathon trail, on the other hand, lets you descend to the roads of Afon Mawddach, right next to the river, which brings you into the Afron Wen valley. The run has some good elevation changes and ends with a climb up the Cefndeuddwr ridge to get back to the visitor center. The running trails vary in completion time from about half an hour to 4 hours and numerous levels of difficulty so that both the novice and the experienced runner can enjoy themselves.

A more strenuous trail also exists, the Gain Waterfall Trail, which goes over forest roads, uneven surfaces, and muddy portions that take you to the Cefndeuddwr ridge. Then you reach the next valley, which brings you down to where the Afon Mawddach and Afon Gain Rivers meet along with their waterfalls, providing you with the much-needed serenity and scenic beauty after traversing through the hectic terrain.

Chapter 20: Battlefields and Borderlands Way

If you are passionate about history and love running, what better way to bring those two seemingly unrelated aspects together into a walk that is the brainchild of two Bosworth Battlefield Heritage Center guides? This 68-kilometer long circular trail that loops between Warwickshire and Leicestershire is designed to take you through sites that let you explore 2000 years of English history.

The traditional starting and ending point for the walk is the Witherley Church in Leicestershire. The best way to enjoy the trail is to have the accompanying guidebook of the same name, which describes in great detail, the history of each of the places that you will be going through on your journey. While 68 kilometers cannot be run in a single stretch, segments of the trail can be converted into running segments that explore the various historical sites. The main attraction of this route happens to be the place where the Battle of Bosworth was fought, which was a civil war between the Houses of Lancaster and York. Interestingly, the site might also be the one that saw yet another major historical moment – the defeat of the rebel Boudica by the Roman Army in Roman Britain in AD 60 or 61. As you run by these now vast stretches of greenery, you cannot help but think of what these places have seen – the iconic moments that undoubtedly shaped today's world.

The trail visits other areas of historical turmoil, notably two Civil War locations; one has seen a siege while the other – a cavalry skirmish. It also covers more recent history as it passes through a reconstructed Royal Air Force tower and a nuclear bunker that was built during the Cold War era. It also enables you to be in touch with rural England as it goes through about 20 villages and a market town, as well as an abandoned village. The entire route is well signposted as it mostly makes use of public footpaths and occasionally small roads and pavements, ideal for running and jogging. The book is a must accompaniment, which describes not only historical events but also notable people who lived in the area along with illustrations and a range of photographs. While quite testing on endurance owing to the running segments interspersed between the walking segments, the trail is a historical refresher which you will enjoy a lot.

Chapter 21: The Pembrokeshire Coastal Path

This trail is designated as a national one located in Pembrokeshire in the southwest of Wales. Earlier, people used to call this pathway the "Land of Mystery and Enchantment" for its surreal beauty. It is a 299 Km (186 miles) long route with spectacular scenic views and includes several twists and turns throughout the journey. The highest elevation point is at Camas Head at 574 ft (175 meters). This trail can be visited during any season of the year. The pathway was established on 16th May 1970 by Wynford Vaughan Thomas.

This national trail covers a vast range of topography and physical features - from open-sea beaches, glacial valleys, steep cliffs made of limestone to red sandstone structures. The route passes through 58 beaches in all. A significant saga of birdlife is seen during the early summers and spring seasons. A number of migratory birds can be found here during the winters. European seabirds are abundant, whereas offshore, dolphins and seals can be found. Several pieces of evidence of the bronze age can be found here. The trail is a bit strenuous owing to the innumerable undulations, which makes it a physical constraint for many. There are adequate bus and car services to and from the trail. Various popular locations are situated in the pathway, such as St. Dogmaels, Dinas Island, Whitesands Bay, Pembroke Dock, Wiseman's Bridge, and many more. The surrounding land is primarily used for agriculture and farming, and fishing is prevalent near the shores. In the year 2011, the Pembrokeshire path found themselves in National Geographic Magazine when they voted into the second-best coastal path. People from all over the globe visit this trail, and each of them finds it astonishingly beautiful.

Chapter 22: The Jurassic Coast

This is a World Heritage site in the Southern part of England. It extends from Exmouth in Devon (East) to Dorset. The stretch is about 154 Km (96 miles) in length. It is an ancient site of about 185 million years of geographical history. The weather is severe here at times. Few violent storms had destroyed some cliffs causing not only structural damage but also flooding of the coastal areas. On 15th April 2021, the biggest rockfall collapse in the United Kingdom happened at the Jurassic Coast. Hence, this coast is always prone to erosions, landslides, and natural disasters. Shipwrecks are also a common disaster in the sea harbors that come under this coast.

The Jurassic Coast encompasses cliffs of different geological time periods; Triassic, Jurassic, and Cretaceous. This site was covered in swamps during the Cretaceous, was a part of a sea during Jurassic, and a dessert during Triassic. The point of highest elevation on this coast as well as in entire south Britain is Golden Cap which is 627 ft (191 meters). This site is popular for exhibiting brilliant kinds of landform, such as the arch at the door of Durdle, limestone folding at the caves of Lulworth. Several fossil-based evidence is found that helps us know about the region's type of animals, flora, and fauna. There is a fossil forest in Lulworth Caves comprising fossils of cycads and conifers. There are sandstone structures that are brilliantly carved. The site was designated to be a World Heritage site in the year 2001. Hundreds of visitors visit the place every year, making it one of the most popular sites in England. A run along this coast is a run through the pages of ancient history, the rich cultural heritage, and enormous, beautiful structures.

Chapter 23: Wherryman's Way, Norfolk

Wherryman's way is a route extending from Norwich to Great Yarmouth. It is a 56 Km (35 miles) long route passing through several lakes, gardens, and markets. The pathway is named after wherries that used River Yare for their journey to the shores of Norwich. Various small picturesque villages make the way even more attractive. The path proceeds along the River Yare alongside. During winters, the trail is comparatively empty, while in summers, the Yare river is crowded with cruises, boats, and tourists. It's a very popular tourist spot attracting people from all over the globe. The walk will take you through some of the most magnificent views of Norfolk. There are sufficient means of accommodation and facilities so that the tourists can have a comfortable and pleasant stay. The weather here is usually pleasant in general but unpredictable at the same time. At times, a sudden downpour can interfere with your prior plans.

A number of beautiful, vibrant migratory and local birds are found here, especially during summers, such as Egyptian geese, barn owl, etc. Buckingham comes in the way, which is famous for the thatched roof of the church of St. Gregory. The Golden Sands at Great Yarmouth is another major attraction of this journey. A few years ago, this trail was flooded by the Yare river, and hence the flood-defense work is going on at the riverside. If you are fond of countryside views, Wherryman's Way is undoubtedly the best you can get in the area.

Chapter 24: West Highland Way

It's a long pathway located in Scotland. This route is a challenging one owing to its long stretch of 154 Km (96 miles). This is Scotland's first officially recognized long walking route, established in the year of 1980. The weather is not that favorable here, reaching extremes. The highest elevation point is at Kinghouse, which is 1800 ft. (550 meters) high. The route extends from north Glasgow to Scottish Highlands. The trail can be used for running, walking, hiking, biking, and horse riding as well. At some portions of the trail, due to a large number of visitors, the land has eroded. A few places need renovation at the earliest, but that's minuscule. Few of the most iconic features in the landscape are found here.

Remarkable wildlife features can be seen, including golden eagles, feral goats, red deer, etc. The trail passes through some famous villages and towns like Fort William, Bridge of Orchy, Drymen, Tyndrum, etc. Another noticeable fact about West Highland Way is that it is used for marathons and ultramarathons. Majorly three races are held annually – The West Highland Way Race of 153 Km (95 miles) covering the whole Highland Way from north to South, The Highland Fling Race of 85 Km (53 miles) starting from Milngavie ending at Tyndrum, The Devil o' the Highlands footrace of 69 Km (43 miles). Several rural communities and villages add to the attraction of the place. A surplus amount of hotel facilities are present for the tourists. This trail is an absolute recommendation for scenic beauty, picturesque villages, notable wildlife and birds, and challenging climbs.

Chapter 25: Race to the Stones

Race to the Stones is recognized as the oldest path of Britain. It is a 100 Km route with incredibly scenic views, along with remnants of ancient history. The route is a challenging one starting from Oxfordshire and ending Avebury Stone Circle. Avebury Stone Circle is a popular Neolithic structure that is nearly five thousand years old.

Various marathons and races are conducted here, and a number of athletes participate. The terrain is hilly, and a few hazards like flints, stones, tree roots, hidden ruts, etc. It is an amazing experience to hike on this trail.

Chapter 26: Westonbirt Arboretum, Gloucestershire

It is a botanical collection mostly of trees located in Gloucestershire, England. It was created in 1829 by Robert Stayner Holford. Later, his son, George Lindsay Holford, extended the arboretum and also facilitated various developments of the route. In 1956, the arboretum got assigned under the supervision of the Forestry of England. This arboretum is listed as a Grade I arboretum under Special parks of historical interest. This stretch of 5 Km (3 miles) might seem a limited area by distance, but it is the most popular and most beautiful arboretum in the United Kingdom.

Westonbirt Arboretum contains around 15000 shrubs and trees covering a wide area of nearly 600 acres. There is a wide variety of unique or rare plants here. A major attraction of the arboretum is the Silkwood house. It is a unique experience here. Silkwood house is a sort of property containing exotic plant varieties and a woodland in the center which is of 13th century. One should definitely go for the Silkwood house if they visit this arboretum.

Chapter 27: Wendover Woods, Buckinghamshire

In the northern side of Chiltern Hills of England, a woodland area was named the Wendover Woods. The name Wendover was given after a town which is located nearby. The maximum elevation point is 876 ft., and the area covered is 800 acres. It is a bridleway and is filled with coniferous trees. The countryside views are absolutely breathtaking, and the weather is usually pleasant here without any disturbances. The woods are under the surveillance of the Forestry of England.

The facilities here are abundant in all regards, be it food, accommodation or transportation. This trail is not the challenging or exhausting one; it's an ordinary route with some extraordinary views and sights. This place gives you the peace of mind that you lack amidst the race and pace of city life. The Aston Hill Mountain, Aylesbury Vale, and some stone monuments are few remarkable attractions of this trail.

Chapter 28: Mallards Pike, Forest of Dean

In the western part of Gloucestershire, Lydney in the Forest of Dean lies Mallards Pike. It is of triangular shape. The birdsong here is a major attraction, owing to the presence of innumerable exotic bird varieties. Several different kinds of lizards are also found here. The Pike is surrounded by various sorts of trees making the whole site absolutely beautiful.

Races and marathons are conducted here of stretches 5 Km and 10 Km. The forest is beside the rivers Wye and River Severn. This place is an ideal vacation location due to the rivers, plenty of exotic bird varieties, and lots of greenery. The forest can be visited during any season but might cause trifle disturbances during the rainy season. This is because there is a steep downhill road near the end of the forest, which is not surfaced and can be muddy. The pathway comprises dismantled railway parts before entering the deeper forest. But, in all, if hazards are taken care of, Mallards Pike should be on your list.

Chapter 29: Alice Holt, Surrey

A rich oak forest located in Farnham, Surrey, covers a huge area of nearly 2142 acres. This forest is a major attraction, and around 250 thousand visitors visit the place in a year. A brilliant tourist spot for each and everyone with adequate means and modes of transport. The nearest railway station to the forest is the Bentley which is 2 miles from there. This forest has been under the supervision of the Forestry Commission body since the year of 1924. Every Saturday, a marathon of 5 Km is held in which hundreds of athletes take part. This event of marathon is held at Bucks Horn Oak, Hampshire. The pathway is a bridleway. Hence it is suitable for running. The forest can be visited during any season of the year. But, the place can be a little muddy at times owing to the unpredictable downpour.

Various marathons and other events are arranged here by the local volunteers. To join the marathon, you need to register beforehand, even though it's free for all. The roads are primarily made of gravel and tarmac. It is mixed terrain. It's hilly and sloppy in some areas, while in others, it's mostly plain, and rarely you might come across eroded muddy areas. The oak tree shade, the pleasant weather, and the picturesque beauty of the place are surely going to add a memorable experience to your travel diaries.

Chapter 30: Bedgebury National Pinetum and Forest, Kent

It is located at Bedgebury, Kent, in the United Kingdom. Ten thousand specimens of conifers are found here. 5 Km and 10 Km race events are held where hundreds of participants take part. These races start at Gruffalo Hill point and later enter the deeper forest. The forest can be visited during any time of the year.

There are beautiful woods, picturesque scenic views, and plenty of rare plant species. It's a treat to the eyes to be amidst so much greenery. The 5 Km and 10 Km routes meet at a point downhill where it merges into a marshal lake. Overall, the beauty of the place is unparalleled, and it holds unending charms despite the simple route. For runners, walkers, hikers, and even bikers, the place is an ideal one. But, one should take safety measures throughout the journey to avoid unwanted hazards.

Chapter 31: Haldon Forest Park, Devon

Haldon Forest Park, located just 15 minutes from Exeter in Devon, has something for everyone, whether you're looking for a peaceful run or a thrilling mountain bike adventure. Haldon Forest and its 3500 acres of woodlands have a variety of walking and cycling trails for people of all abilities, as well as a pump loop, bike skills area, orienteering courses, and much more.

Haldon Forest Park Forest, which has a café and a variety of trails and activities, is a great place for groups to participate in a variety of learning activities ranging from den construction to orienteering that mix hands-on learning with ideas for active minds. Through hands-on activities, you can learn more about how forests are managed sustainably for wildlife, people, and timber.

The forest park is rich in accessible amenities starting with the Ridge Café, which is open daily and offers outdoor seating and a takeaway option as well. The place is also friendly for dogs, which makes it an ideal place to visit for a picnic with your favorite canine. Apart from running trails, mountain biking trails and guides are also available, as well as horse riding courses and classes. Haldon Forest Park shapes up to be an ideal place for a short weekend getaway to be a bit closer to nature but not completely off the grid. The running trails are thoroughly waymarked and make it easily accessible for people wanting to enjoy a run through the forest.

Chapter 32: Salcey Forest, Northamptonshire

Many kilometers of historic wood banks, building ruins, and ancient trees can be found in the Salcey Forest, located about 11km from Northampton. The druids, also known as veteran oaks, are a rare and spectacular animal habitat, with some of the old oaks dating back over 600 years. The medieval royal hunting woodland has unique secrets that it offers to its various patrons.

The park offers numerous activities for visitors to indulge in. Apart from the 3 fantastic walking trails, a cycling trail, a horse riding trail, archery, and ax-throwing activities and picnic areas are available, catering to the interests of a varied group of people, making it an ideal place for a family or office expedition. The park is also dog friendly and has a café.

While there are no exclusive running trails, the walking trails are used as running trails, and there is also a park running event. To promote running, the park has its own "Salcey Forest Runners" Strava group, where you can record your lap times and see where you land on the leaderboard versus the other runners!

The elephant walk trail provides a short run through the woods to the elephant pond, which got its name during WWII when elephants from a traveling circus were utilized to remove falling trees from the forest. After a hard day's labor, the elephants were allowed to bathe in the pond, and the pond became famed for its huge bathers. Other trails include the Church Path Trail and the Woodpecker trail, the latter being the longest one. All trails offer a spectacular journey through woodlands while being able to experience the diverse wildlife that the place has to offer – common lizards, deer, bird species native to Salcey, as well as foxes.

Chapter 33: Delamere Forest, Northwich

If the city life is becoming too much for you and you are desperately in need of a break, away from the urban cacophony and into the heart of nature, a shady oasis just southwest of Manchester might be the place to visit. Easy-going pathways for all levels, a hike to admire the view across to Liverpool's famed skyline, orienteering courses for all abilities, or a bit of quiet to watch the wildlife around the lake are all accessible via Delamere's very own train station. Forest Holidays has a variety of beautiful forest cottages that are ideal for getting away from it all.

The forest offers several walking trails, which double as running trails, two cycling trails, and a Go Ape outdoor adventure if you are not afraid of heights, a Segway if you are apart from being furnished with basic amenities such as restrooms, cafes, and a bike hiring station. It is also dog-friendly if you want to take some time off with your favorite pets.

The three offered trails are all quite short, not extending beyond 5 kilometers, and offer spectacular scenery of the British woodlands. All the running trails are way marked. The Blakemere trail takes you to the Blakemere Moss, a lake that happens to be an ideal spot for bird watching or just being in the laps of nature. The Linmere trails are ideal for a family-run, passing through the woods along with Blakemore Moss, while the Old Pale Trail, although incorporating a significant amount of ascent than the other two trails, will reward you with beautiful views of the skyline.

Chapter 34: Sherwood Pines, Nottinghamshire

Being one of the most well-known forests in the Midlands, Sherwood Pines boasts of an amazing array of activities that you can do while being closer to nature. The forest offers three walking and 3 cycling trails, 2 running trails that span 5 and 10 kilometers, fun activities such as disc golf and bushcrafting, as well as orienteering services for folks who would like to get more serious about camping or hiking. The forest also offers a majestic tree to tree zipline experience with Go Ape as well as Nordic walking and forest Segway. Sherwood Pines can also be enjoyed much more casually as a family outing thanks to its picnic area, which is dog friendly, and its café.

The running trails, one 5 km, and the other 10 km allow you to experience the best of Sherwood Pines. The 5 km circular route covers Pines and Broadleaf vegetation across the forest on mixed terrain, with soft under the footing, although muddy at times. The 10 km route starts to like the 5 km route but splits up at the 2 km point to take you to the Robin Hood's Whetstone past Tornado Alley. The trail covers pines and broadleaf and makes its way to the outer parts of the forest before rendezvousing with the 5 km trail after 7 km.

Chapter 35: Dalby Forest, North Yorkshire

The Dalby Forest is a really good place to go on the typical forestry activities that you might undertake somewhere else, such as hiking, cycling, or ziplining through the trees. However, what makes the forest stand apart from other forests are its skies rather than its landscape. The Dalby Forest is a designated Dark Sky Discovery Site which means the skies here are so clear that you can see our galactic home, the Milky Way, through your naked eyes.

During the daytime, when there is not much astrophysics to be done unless you happen to be a heliophysics enthusiast, bothered with the workings of the sun, the Dalby Forest is as pristine as the views that it offers during the evening. Comprising of a uniquely rugged and dale landscape between glacial valleys and an upland plateau which offers amazing forest adventures all year round. It offers about 13 walking trails, 4 running and cycling trails, Go Ape tree ziplining facilities, and campsites to facilitate stargazing activities at night. The area is dog friendly with a café available.

The running trails include two 5 km trails, a 3 km running route, and a 10 km trail. The 3 km route is ideal for beginners with turnaround points if you are too fatigued. The Ellerburn trail is a 5 km route, circular, making use of the forest roads and passing through the oldest portions of the forest. The running route allows you to experience the beautiful waters of the Dalby Beck before returning along the Low Dalby Valley. The Adderstone trail, also clocking in at 5 km, takes you to the Adderstone field, where you can inspect naturally sculpted adder stone from prehistoric times. Finally, the Staindale running route is a circular 10 km long trail that goes across Yondhead Rigg, Crosscliff, and some parts of the Jerry Noodle trail, for the most part on forest roads and sometimes on some feature paths of interest. This trail offers some spectacular views across the New York Moors.

Chapter 36: Whinlatter Forest, Cumbria

If you love forests as well as mountains and you are a person who simply cannot compromise between these two, then maybe it's time to pay a visit to England's only mountain forest – the Whinlatter Forest, a World Heritage Site located in the Lake District. It offers majestic views across Bassenthwaite Lake, Derwentwater, and Keswick and offers amazing trails to explore more of the scenic beauty that has instilled and inspired creativity in many souls.

The forest offers walking and running trails as wells as cycling trails, ziplining, and forest Segway. Bikes and mobility scooters can be hired from the visitor's center, which also has play areas and a café as well as a forest shop.

The running trails, 5 and 10 kilometers long as well as the walking trails take you through the forest path along a gradual ascent to viewpoints such as "Bob's Seat" or "Seat How" while enjoying the conifers and the wildlife of the region, of which the most notable mentions go to the red squirrel and the roe deer. The park also offers a "park run" for groups of people as well as a running club. The 10 km running route takes you to the solitary portions of the forest with two big climbs, one towards Seat How and the other through a coniferous portion of the forest which leads the way downhill to Revelin Moss, before completing a section alongside Grisedale Gill and back to the visitor center.

Chapter 37: Cannock Chase Forest, Staffordshire

Located just north of Birmingham, the Cannock Chase Forest will be your go-to destination if you are craving a little closeness with nature along with your loved ones. A plethora of activities are offered here, including walking and running trails in addition to Go Ape zip lines and forest Segway. The park also has a café, is dog friendly, and offers a dog trail and other fun activities such as treetop climbing and horse riding.

Running routes are way marked and range from 3 kilometers to 10 kilometers. The running routes allow you to immerse yourself in the peace and tranquility of the forest while listening to the nightjars and woodlarks at its heart. Places of interest include a model railway crossing and the Fairoak pools. Some trails are more challenging due to their incline and challenging terrain underfoot, comprising of pebbles or mud, and allows amateur and seasoned runners to find something challenging. The forest is also a selected venue for the 2022 Commonwealth Games mountain biking event, giving you enough impetus to rent one and try it out for yourself! The park also engages in outreach activities promoting general fitness, and mental health awareness in the form of Junior Park Runs as well as "RunTalkRun" events that take place weekly every Sunday at 10 AM. They are a great place to meet people from different walks of life and come together as a community.

Chapter 38: High Willhays, Dartmoor

The highest point of South England might not sound like much, but a run across the High Willhays will be worth your efforts for sure. Clocking in at about 13 kilometers from the impressive Meldon Dam built in the year 1972, your run will bring you close to nature and a live firing range that the military actively uses for about 200 years! Dartmoor's bleak yet stunning and beautiful rocky landscape is unparalleled and enjoyable in solitude, and the skies are vast and never-ending. You might come across trig points with radio masts used in the early 30s to make more accurate maps of this part of England using radios and trigonometry, a fascinating relic of how maps used to be made in those days!

The High Willhays is quite rocky, desolate, and windy and a perfect place to collect your thoughts and arrange some volcanic granite stones into small monuments as the wind howls in your ears. You can spend some time taking a break from your run here and return along the West Okement River and visit other parts of the area such as the Meldon viaducts and marvel at their engineering marvels.

Chapter 39: The Basingstoke Canal Towpath Trail

If you are looking for a run full of scenic beauty through the English countryside, the Basingstoke Canal walk is something that should be up on your to-do list. Clocking in at around 53 kilometers, the path runs through numerous villages of Surrey and Hampshire and is good for hikers and cyclists who want to have a day or two amid nature. The terrain is flat and relatively easy to run on, going from West Byfleet in Surrey to Greywell in Hampshire with a visitor center at the halfway point, which has restrooms and a café. Additionally, hiring a boat and camping are also allowed between Easter and the month of September.

As you run down the trail, the clear waters of the canal make it easy to see the various aquatic plants. There are numerous species of dragonflies in the area that might be of interest to a budding entomologist. Along the trail, several historical sites and buildings are visible such as the Odiham Castle, scenic aqueducts, and the picturesque villages of rural England. The trail is a green corridor connecting to other trails, so don't be shy to start a mini adventure of your own! The villages being interspersed along the way make for an ideal running setting where you can have running segments from one village to the next one before resting and moving onto the next running segment.

Chapter 40: The Tarka Trail

Taking its name from the titular character in Henry Williamson's novel, the Tarka trail is a 290 km trail for walking, running, and cycling that will let you explore North Devon in its sheer glory. A portion of the trail also allows horse riding. The trail covers a variety of landscapes – coastal beaches, moorlands, river valleys, and cliffs. The entire trail is a figure-eight loop, centered on Barnstaple, and has numerous places to stay, including hotels, campsites, and B&Bs. Numerous restaurants, delis, and pubs are also available along the trail.

The Tarka Trail passes over some truly spectacular Devon features, such as the Crow Point, which happens to be the conjunction between two estuaries going into the sea. The south loop of the trail runs through Eggesford Forest, which has its railway station. The forest links several other kinds of wood together and is an enchanting atmosphere for a family excursion while staying in a cottage. You can have local circular runs here as well.

To ensure visitors get adequate information about the history and heritage of particular sites, the trail includes 21 yellow-topped audio posts spread along its length, which has an information plaque and a QR code. Scanning the code will enable the runners to learn more about the history and wildlife of the associated area. Have a taste of the best of England while running or cycling along this iconic trail.

Chapter 41: Putsborough to Woolacombe Beach Run

Woolacombe Beach is an award-winning beach and one of the best beaches in the UK. If you like to take a run along the beach, then this area is perfect for you. You can get a nearly 5 K run in along Woolacombe beach. It is a fairly straightforward route, so all you have to concentrate on is the challenge of running on sand without having to think about getting off the trail.

You will begin in the Putsborough car park and then head towards the beach and follow it along to Woolacombe. After you get there, you can either head back along the same path, or you can use public transit to take you back to the starting point.

Each Saturday morning, there is often a Woolacombe Dunes Park Run that starts at 9 AM. Given the fact that you have dunes, the terrain will be varied, giving you a bit of a challenge.

Chapter 42: Clifton Down, Bristol

Clifton Down is a public space in Bristol, just north of the village of Clifton. Its neighbor, Durdham Down at the northeast, makes up an area known as the Downs. This area is used for many different leisure activities.

Clifton Downs is a vast grassy area that provides you with ample area to run, with many different footpaths. From the top of Westbury Hill to the Sea wall and around the Spire hospital and returning to Westbury, you will have a fairly flat route that will give you about a four-mile loop.

In the Downs, you also have a 5 K loop in the greenest grass in Bristol. It provides you with panoramic views that stretch the Avon valley. It is a very flat area, so it is great for those who aren't a fan of climbing hills.

Chapter 43: West Bay, Dorset

When you are at West Bay, you have crumbling golden cliffs of sand that allow you to see sea levels that have fallen some 175 million years ago. There is an 18 mile long Chesil Beach that was created from landslides that eroded away at the end of the last ice age, about 20,000 years ago.

There are two beaches on West Bay. East Beach is a well-visited beach that is backed by the stunning East Cliff. Then there is West Beach, which isn't visited as much. Both are great shingle beaches.

There is a five-mile route along with the village of West Bay in Dorset. It is a fairly flat route that allows you to enjoy some beautiful golden cliffs and lovely beaches. The walk begins at the harbor at West Bay. This is also called Bridport Harbour. From here, you will head east past the Gold Club and head towards Burton Bradstock. It will take you through the village before you descend to Burton Beach. In this area, you will pick up part of the South West Coast Path. This can then be followed back to West Bay.

If you want to extend your run, you can head east along the beach towards Weymouth and the Isle of Portland.

Chapter 44: Box Hill, Surrey

Box Hill is a great place to discover and explore Surrey Hills. It forms part of the North Downs, and it has amazing views of the surrounding countryside. It is also home to a whole host of plants and wildlife.

There are a number of routes that you can run in the Box Hill area. One of the easiest routes to take is the hilltop stroll. It is just a one-mile run that starts at the visitor center and the top of box hill. Don't take the right path. Go along the surfaced path that runs with the road, then head down the steps or slope and take a right and follow the path. Don't take the left-hand path. Instead, go uphill to the right. Follow the path downhill, past Peter Labilliere's gravestone. Then take the stony track and back to the visitor center.

If you like a run with some elevation, you can take the eight-mile circular run that covers much of the Box Hill estate. It starts at the Box Hill Shepherd's Hut and then heads for Lodge Hill. Follow the path to Broadwood's Folly, and you will go through another car park. You'll take steps up to Mickleham Down, then turn left at the T-junction towards the Mickleham village. Head towards the old Roman Road of Stane Street. Keep following the trail around back to where you started.

One more route you can take is 2.7 miles long and starts at the visitor center. Follow the signs toward Broadwood's tower and then head down to Happy Valley. You'll turn right at point three and walk-up Happy Valley. Once you're at the top, follow the main path that takes you to the road. At the restaurant, cross the road, go right, and then walk through the woods to North Downs Way. Then follow on through to return to the visitor center.

Chapter 45: Calder Valley, Yorkshire

The Calder Valley is in West Yorkshire and includes the towns of Sowerby Bridge, Luddendenfoot, Mytholmroyd, Hebden Bridge, and Todmorden. This is the upper valley of the River Calder. This falls entirely within the larger metropolitan area of Calderdale.

There are a number of running trails in the Calder Valley, and there are many towns in the area that take part in the "Walkers are Welcome" club. Whether you want a short and easy run or something that is more strenuous, there are a number of trails that you can take.

There is a Mary Towneley Loop that takes a 47-mile section of the Pennine Bridleway and has a variety of tracks that loop past Blackshaw Head, Walsden, Todmorden, Hebden Bridge, and Heptonstall.

A great area to go running is in Calderdale Way. It is 50 miles of valleys, hills, and moors that you can explore. It is a very up and down journey that has a couple of level sections. This area encircles Todmorden, Hebden Bridge, and Halifax.

You can also take the Todmorden Centenary Way. It is a 20-mile circular route that you can join in on at any point and taken in any order you would like. It will take you through steep-sided valleys, open moors, woodland, and pastures.

There are a number of other paths you can take that cater to all experience levels.

Chapter 46: Elan Valley, Powys, Mid Wales

Elan Valley is a river valley in Powys, located in the Welsh Lake District. It spans over 70 square miles. It contains the Elan Valley Reservoirs and Elan Village. Whether you are into something easy or a challenge, you can find it in Elan. People have open access to most of the 70 square miles of land. There are more than 80 miles worth of designated rights of way.

For an easy path to take, you can do the Cnwch Wood. It is a mile long and is a gentle, well-surfaced terrain. Then you have the Elan Valley Trail. It starts in Rhayader and is nine miles long. It takes you along the old Birmingham Corporation Railway.

If you like a run with some elevation, you can try Craig Cnwch. It starts at the visitor center and is 3.5 miles long. It has steep climbs of 40 meters up steps and 140 meters over the entire run. Another trail that will give you some elevation is the Gro Wood that starts in Llannerch y Cawr Car Park. It is 4.5 miles long and has a steady climb of 170 meters, plus three streams to cross.

For a 6.5 mile run, you could take the Garreg Ddu Reservoir route that starts at the Llanerchi Car Park. It doesn't have any significant climbs, but there are some areas that have wet underfoot and narrow paths with exposed tree routes.

The two toughest trails are the Drygarn Fawr and Maen Serth and Crygyn Ci trails. They are both 9.5 miles long. Drygarn Fawr starts in the Llannerc y Cawr car park and will take you to the highest point of the Elan Estate at 2,104 feet.

The Maen Serth trail starts in Penbont Cark Park and has four climbs. There are a short steep 25 meters climb over 100 meters of the trail. Then you have a 180-meter climb ever 1.5 km. Then a 50-meter climb over 1 km and a 100 meter climb over 1 km. There are also two streams that will have to be crossed.

Chapter 47: The Kerry Way

The Kerry Way comes in at just over 200 kilometers, making it one of Ireland's longest signposted walking trails. It is also one of the most popular. The start of the trail can be found in Killarney, a popular tourist area. It loops around the Iveragh Peninsula, and takes a counterclockwise direction, and takes you through some isolated and dramatic countryside areas.

Kerry is most well known for having the highest mountains in Ireland. When you take the Kerry Way, it will help you avoid some of the higher peaks, and instead, you will get to experience some of the lower reaches of the mountain ridges. The trial will take you quickly through a number of different landscapes and experiences, which will help expand your appreciation for the county.

The Kerry Way is a long trail and cannot be consumed all in one day. It is most commonly broken down into nine stages and ran over a nine-day period. However, this can be extremely demanding if you are not experienced in ultra running.

The terrain you can expect to experience along the Kerry Way includes tarmac roads to rugged roads and even to the wild mountainous countryside. It also takes roads to know to the Irish as "boreens," which are long-abandoned coach roads that have become overgrown with grass. There are some sections that also take you through forestry, farmland, and national parks, which can get boggy.

If you walk the entire Kerry Way, you will get to see things like the Torc Waterfall, Galway's Bridge, and more. In some areas, you can expect an ascent of 300 meters or more.

It is important to be aware of what the weather is supposed to be like during the time you plan on taking the Kerry Way. If you are journeying at any time from late fall to early spring, this is the best time for the most unfavorable weather. You could experience rain, snow, and sleet, along with freezing temperatures. Add in the fewer daylights hours, and this could prove to be a challenging undertaking.

Chapter 48: Monarchs Way

This trail is one of the longest of all English long-distance footpaths. It follows along the path that Prince Charles II took when he was fleeing to France after his army was beaten at the Battle of Worcester during the English Civil War in 1651. It is a 615-mile journey that ends in West Sussex at Shoreham-by-Sea.

It is a slightly random and meandering path that reflects the precarious situation that Charles found himself in. He took off, heading south to Somerset and then off to Dorset. The entire route is waymarked with a logo of a ship above the crown of Charles.

From the start in Worcester, it travels north to Boscobel and then moves towards Stratford Upon Avon. It then moves to Stow on the Wold before heading towards Bristol. Then you head towards Somerset before turning south west to Charmouth. Then you turn north towards Yeovil. Then it takes you to the escarpment of Cranborne Chase. It ends at Brighton and Hove.

If you don't want to undertake the entire Monarch's Way footpath, you can choose to do any section of the path that you want. Since the path is so well marked, it shouldn't be a problem for most people to find their way. However, to be on the safe side, there are a number of guides that you can find to use.

Chapter 49: Druid's Challenge Trail

If you are up for a challenge, then you can try out the druid's challenge trail. This is an 84-mile ultra adventure that takes you through the historic Ridgeway. Each year, runners can choose to push themselves to the limit and do the three-day race, or you can choose to run only one day of the three-day event.

It is located in Tring Park Cricket Club in London. Runners who take this trail will follow in the footsteps of soldiers, travelers, and herdsmen who have used the Ridgeway since prehistoric times.

The 84 miles is spread over a three-day competition where each day you run 28 miles. The first leg of the race will take you through Wendover and Wendover Woods. The event organizers have accommodations set up for the runners at Icknield Community College at the end of day one unless you get a hotel. The second leg takes you past the River Thames and Goring. Once you finish the race on the third day, you will end in Swindon.

This race is not for the faint of heart. If you choose to do this race, you will be given plenty of information on the route and the things that you need to watch out for. It is held in November, so be sure to pack accordingly.

Chapter 50: Hell of A Hill Marathon – Chorley

If you are looking for a challenge, then this is the marathon for you. It is a favorite of many marathon runners and even for some newbies. It is recognized as one of the toughest courses and is a five-day event for those that love endurance and are willing to run the course five times.

This event has people striving to complete five consecutive marathons around one of the toughest 26.2-mile routes in the UK on five consecutive days. It has a 30,000-foot elevation gain and tough terrain. It is located on Bibbys Farm in Chorley, UK.

You start out at Bibby's Farm and head 3.5 miles out towards the feed station on a country road route. Then you will do five laps of 3.85 miles over Rivington Pike, which has a water and food station at the end of every lap. Then you take the original 3.5-mile loop back to the HQ. You will climb over 4,000 feet in each race.

This event will take place in November every year, which means you will have exposed terrain, and there is a good chance of potential extreme weather. In past years, there have been snow, flooding, winds, and extremely cold temperatures. Race HQ will give you updates each day, and the race could be cancel because of extreme weather.

Chapter 51: Lulworth Cove Trail

The Lulworth cove area was created by the combined forces of the sea and a river filled with melting ice during the last Ice Age. It is well known for its unique geology and landforms, which include the Stair Hole and Lulworth Crumple.

There are a network of Permissive footpaths and other walkways that allow you to explore the estate and coast. If starting in West Lulworth, you can take the "South West Coast Path" or the "Purbeck Way West."

The South West Coast Path is an 11.5-mile point-to-point trail that is located near Weymouth, Dorset. It has an elevation gain of 2,011 feet.

There are also a number of circular trails you can take that come in various intensities and sceneries. These trails are marked on the maps and guides that are available at the Lulworth Visitor Centre. Please be mindful of any cliffs that you try to walk on. Some are crumbling and dangerous. Any gates that you open, please close behind you. If you take your dog with you, please keep them on a leash, especially where livestock is present and during the nesting season.

Chapter 52: Glen Coe, Highlands

Glen Coe is located within the Lochaber Geopark. This is an amazing scenic area and serves as the backdrop for the areas macabre history, the Macdonalds massacre. This is often a Mecca for the avoid runners. One of the highest peaks in this area is the Bidean Nam Bian, and it is known as the "three sisters."

The South is the secluded and quiet area of the Glen Etive and has its own impressive mountain ranges. North and east of this area are Loch Leven. There are trails in this area that range from 2 kilometers long to 150 kilometers long. The grade for each trial also varies greatly.

The longest route is the West Highland Way and has to be taken in eight stages. It is well-waymarked and avoids the high tops. The grade is not too rough, but the distance is what you have to watch out for.

The toughest route to take would be Aonach Eagach. It is the narrowest ridge on the mainland. This route is a grade 2/3 scramble and is considered a "moderate" rock climb. It comes in at 9.5 kilometers and has an ascent of 1100 meters.

A moderate trail would be the Two Lairigs. It is a circular walk that combines two historic passes between Glen Etive and Glen Coe. It has good hill paths and is about 15 kilometers long. There are some areas that, at times, are impassable. Some areas are boggy, and the Military Road in Glen Coe is often waterlogged and boggy.

Chapter 53: Aberfoyle to Comrie

A popular running route is a route between Aberfoyle and Comrie. This is part of the Scottish National Trail and is broken into two sections. The first section is the stretch from Aberfoyle to Callander, which is 9.5 miles. The second stretch is from Callander to Comrie, which is 16.5 miles.

In the first stretch, you climb gently through the forests of Trossachs before you descend back down to Loch Venachar. This section ends in the town of Callander, which has often been called the Gateway to the Highlands. It only has an ascent of about 256 meters. You will face minor roads, forest tracks, and paths. The grade is not that bad, and some of the paths may be indistinct. As far as bogginess goes, most of the walk should be dry, but some sections could be wet.

In the second leg of this route, you will move out of Callander towards the boundary between the Highlands and the Lowlands before heading through Glen Artney to make your Way to Comrie. You will have an ascent of about 614 meters.

The terrain in this section includes paths, tracks, minor roads, as well as nearly pathless, boggy sections. You will face some moderate hillwalks, and you may need to be able to read a map. It can also be very boggy in some sections.

Chapter 54: Ervey – Ness Woods

Ness Country Park is a steep wooded park. It is the remains of natural oakwoods and covers about 50 acres. It has woodland and riverside paths that include footbridges, wooden steps, and several species of birdlife and wildlife. Some recent developments have increased the walk to extend on both sides of the Burntollet River that joins the Every and Ness Woods. It has a level meadow that provides walking access to visitors who might not get around that easily. The park has a visitor's center, wildflower meadows, picnic tables, and wildlife ponds.

The Ervey Woods section extends more than one km on the north side of the river and along the floor of the Burntollet Glen. Since the Burntollet River runs along its south, it is a good walk in every season with only a few inclines. It is best to walk this in spring with all the flowers blooming.

The Burntollet Woods joins the Ness Country Park. These woods are still beginning to grow, but it is an area of interest since it contains pieces of a rare ancient woodland. The Trust has planted more than 43,000 trees here. Most of them are oak with a few wild cherries, alder, and ash. These young trees will slowly link to the ancient woodland. This will give more places for the wonderful wildlife. During the summer, visitors are treated to 27 acres of wonderfully colorful wildflowers. These flowers, along with the oats, barley, and clover, give a wonderful habitat for several species of birds and insects.

To begin the trail, follow the path to the right that begins in the parking lot of the visitor's center. Go past the area of recent ponds and go across Hone's Bridge. Go along the Burntollet River's north side. Don't take the bridge to your right as this is currently closed for renovations. Keep going until you reach another bridge. Go over this bridge and walk up the steps. This path will take you past the Ness waterfall and across Shanes Bridge. Keep going along the path and into the woods; you should go past the viewpoint for the waterfall. Take some time here and enjoy the view.

Keep going along the path downhill until you take a right onto a path that goes uphill. This will lead you above the mature woodland until it reaches a turning point. Take a sharp left down some wooden steps that go to the river. Turn right to get back on the path to go back to the visitors center.

If you take the path to the left of the visitors center, you will cross the Burntollet River near Browns Bridge. Follow this path for one and a half km and turn right at the fork. This route will circle around to Ervey Wood parking lot. Keep going through the parking lot to get to Burntollet Wood. You can follow the red arrows around Burntollet Wood. You are going to see many interesting viewpoints and information panels that talk about the wildflowers and wildlife that you will see along your way. Go through a gate to bypass some private property before you get back into the wood through another gate. Keep following the path back to the Ervey Wood parking lot.

To get back to the visitors center parking lot, cross the small grassland to the right of the parking lot you are in and go into the wood through the wooden gate. This will take you back to the visitors center.

Chapter 55: Volta a McArt's Fort

This rocky hill that overlooks Belfast in Northern Ireland had a highest peak of 368 meters. It has many basalt caves and cliffs. It well know for the feature called "Napoleon's Nose." This is a cliff that looks just like the profile of Napoleon. When you reach the summit, you will find the remains of the McArt's Fort.

This creates part of the Belfast Hills. You can see all of Belfast from the peak. You can also see the Isle of Man and even Scotland if the day is clear. This is located just a couple of miles from the middle of the main city.

It is thought that this was the inspiration for *Gulliver's Travels,* written by Jonathan Swift.

There are three huge caves. The one on the bottom is 21 feet long, goes from seven to ten feet high, and is 18 feet wide. The next cave up is ten feet long, six feet high, and seven feet wide. The cave on top is the biggest cave. It has two parts that aren't equal. Each part of this cave is larger than the other two caves under it. This ascent getting to this cave is very dangerous, and not many people have ventured into it. The caves are man-made, and people believe that they were created to mine iron.

Next to the bottom cave is what is known as "The Devils' Punchbowl." At the top of the cliff if McArt's Fort. At one side of the fort is a steep rock wall, and other side is lined by a ditch. This is very large. The area that is enclosed is almost completely level. The fort's flat top measures 150 feet going from south to north and 180 feet going from west to east. It is thought that the inhabitants of the fort used the caves for food storage during the winter, and they may have used them as a place to hide during attacks.

Chapter 56: Portballintrae – causeway

This is a five-and-a-half-mile circle path along the Causeway Coast. It has a perfect combination of cliff-top views and sandy beaches. This would make a great romantic stroll for any day of the week. Beginning from the parking lot located in Portballintrae at the end of Beach Road, you will follow the trail that goes toward the beach. It will then bear left and go across the Bush River on the Three Quarter Mile Bridge.

From this point, you go turn left and walk along the sand dunes to come out at Runkerry Beach and then keep going along the shore.

Once you are at the top of the beach, you will go left onto a path the goes in front of the Runkerry house. Keep following the path along the cliff top northward. The Runkerry house is a beautiful sandstone house that was built in the early 1860s and used to be part of the Macnaghtens of Dundarave Estate.

You will keep on the path on the coast until you get to the "National Trust's Giant's Causeway Visitors Centre and the Causeway Hotel." You will cross over the building using the grass roof and then walk down the steps to the path the goes down toward the Giants Causeway rock formations before you go along the path to the next bay.

You will turn right at the junction in the path before you reach the rocks called "The Organ" that will take you to Shepherd's Path. Keep on this trail, going up a hill, and then walk up the steps that will take you to the top of the cliff. Take a moment and enjoy the views. At the top of the stairs, stay to the right and go back to the visitors center.

Leave the center by going through the parking lot and turn right at Runkerry Road before it joins Causeway Road. Go about 250 meters into the railway parking lot and turn right. This will join the path that goes away from the station along the railway.

Once the trail starts to move away from the beach, turn right onto a sand dune path until it meets the Bush River. All of the trails through the sand dunes will take you back to the Three Quarter Mile Bridge. You can go across this to get back to the starting point of your walk.

Chapter 57: Greenwich Meridian Trail

This trail was developed in 2009. It follows the line along the Prime Meridian as closely as it can. It only uses public rights in ways. This trail doesn't strictly stay on the Meridian but was chosen to give a memorable, varied, and interesting walk.

The starting point of this trail is the Meridian Monument located at Peacehaven. The trail will then go to South Downs, across to Weald, down through Ashdown Forest, and then across the North Downs. If you are in London, you can avoid walking along the street by using parks, commons, and wooded areas. You can use the Pool at Ravenbourne River and the Green Chain Walk as a way to get to Greenwich. The Greenwich Foot Tunnel will take you north of the river where the Limehouse Cut and Thames Path leads to Stratford and then on to Epping Forest, which is a way out of London that will keep you in nature.

Once you get to Waltham Abbey, the trail will follow the Lea Valley going to Stanstead Abbotts and will continue to the hills of Hertfordshire and on to Cambridgeshire. When you get to Hardwick, you have made it to the halfway point. You will go through Grantchester as this gives you a good access point to the main trail.

The next part of the trail will cross the Fens and pass through March to get to Holbeach and then onto historic Boston. The last part will take you to the wonderful Lincolnshire Wolds and then on to Louth. You will then go to Cleethorpes, which is located on Humber Estuary's south shore. This trail will begin again at the Meridian Marker close to Patrington. From this point, it goes through Withernsea. The trail ends at Sand le Mere. This is where the Meridian will cross the eroding coast in England. A marker has been placed on the cliffs because the Millennium fell to the beach back in 2003.

Chapter 58: Isle of Arran and The Arran Coastal Way

This is a rugged and challenging long-distance trail that runs 109 km around the coast of the Isle of Arran. It will fit neatly into a week-long vacation. The island has a wonderful bus service that makes it possible to walk it in stages from many points along the coast.

Arran is famous for being "Scotland in miniature." It shouldn't surprise you that this trail enjoys wonderful scenery all throughout. This trail doesn't just stay on the coast. It does go inland at many points to sample all the island has to offer you.

It starts with an ascent to Goatfell, but this trail is optional. Goatfell is the island's highest peak. It will give you some wonderful views. From there, you can go through the pretty village of Sannox and Corrie before the trail takes you around the remote of Cock of Arran. Once you get to Lachranza and the ruined castle, the trail will follow an old postman's path to Catacol.

There are trails where you can walk through Pirnmill before the route takes you to King's Cave. The south part of Arran has the hardest part of the route. If you love climbing over boulders, you are going to love the terrain around Dippen Head and Bennan. If these boulders are too hard to get over, there is an easier route. The trail will climb up to Glenashdale Falls from Whiting Bay before it descends back to Lamlash. From here, the trail will stay around the coast for the last stretch going to Brodick.

The coast of Arran has some rugged paths that make it a demanding walk even though there are some low levels at the beginning. There are markers along the way. Yellow stands for the main trail and red for all the alternate routes.

Going up to Goatfell is straight uphill for people who are experienced, but you can stay away from this one by using the alternative routes if you aren't able to do the climb or the weather is bad. There are other sections that are a bit rough along the shore, too. Some don't have a defined path, or it is very swampy, and you might have to climb over a rock or two. The path from Lagg going to Whiting Bay is extremely demanding. It has awkward boulders you have to climb over that are located below both Dippen Head and Bennan Head. If you are near Bennan Head at high tide, you won't be able to go through. Dippen Head will be very rough at high tide. You can avoid both of these places by using alternate routes.

Chapter 59: Suffolk Coast Path

This trail follows a permissive path and rights of ways along the Suffolk Heritage Coast. It will follow the River Ore's western banks and go inland from Orfordness up toward Snape Maltings before you will turn east and go down the north side of the Alde River to get back to the coast while following the festival town called Aldesburgh. From this point, it will follow the coast to Lowestoft South Pier.

It connects to the Orwell and Stour Walk at Felixstowe to take you to Stour Valley Path and the Essex Way at Manningtree. If you are using GPS, it might show these paths as being combined, but they are two different paths.

The Sandlings Walk will take you inland from the path that runs parallel, especially south of Snape, where the route will snake across the forests and heaths. There is a path that will take you back to the coast. Between Southwold and Snape, these two routes will meet and cross several times. Where these two paths meet it gives you many options for some shorter walks.

Chapter 60: Bure Meadows, Bickling

This trail is set in Bure meadows in Norfolk. This trail gives you wonderful views of the beautiful Jacobean mansion located in Blickling. It is surrounded by fields, woods, and parkland and covers a massive 4600 acres. If you visit during spring, the woods will be carpeted with bluebells. There is a trail that is great for pushing buggies or going for a bike ride.

This trail has an abundance of old buildings, trees, and tiny creatures. This estate has several barn owls that you might see hunting in the quiet woods and sometimes even during the day. This trail was created with the help of Sim and Jen Benson, who are expert adventurers and runners. This is part of the Ranger Run Series. This trail does cross the main road two times, so please be careful.

To start this trail, you will go to the Estate Barn visitor center, which is located on Blickling Estate. From the main parking lot, go toward the path that runs parallel to the Estate Barn. You will turn right once you pass the Buckinghamshire Arms pub. This is also the main drive to Blickling.

Once you go along the main path, you should see Blickling Church. You will turn right and go across the road toward Silvergate Lane. Follow the yellow route down Silvergate road. You will turn right onto a small lane once you pass Hall Farm.

When you reach the fork in the road, you will take the left one and then turn left. You will follow it for a short distance until you get to Long Plantation, which will be to your right.

You will now turn right across the road where Brady's Walk joins the multi-user trail. This will be a green route that will have markers along the path. This will go northwest toward Buck's Common. You will go past the Tower.

Continue on this trail and go through Bunkers Hill plantation. The path will curve around toward the Great Woods. Stay on the path toward the Woodgate parking lot and turn right onto Brady's Walk. This will be the yellow path. Follow this path until you come out near the Mausoleum. Now take some time and enjoy the wonderful views across the lake, park, and toward the house.

Once you are at the Mausoleum, take the time to run across the park but stay on the yellow path toward the north part of the lake. Continue to follow the yellow path toward the eastern shore and around the edge of the lake. Then you will turn south and go around the formal gardens. You might see some highlights like Blickling's orangery.

You will come out at the back of the church close to a farmyard. Follow this path south and go past the church, and then you will turn right past the main road again. Go back past the pub and go back to the Estate barn visitor's center to the main parking lot. If you have worked up an appetite, you can grab a bite to eat at Muddy Boots café.

Chapter 61: Castle Drogo, Devon

Castle Drogo is located in Devon, England near Drewsteignton. The castle also has a formal garden. There are a number of winding paths at Castle Drogo that can take you down into the gorge. If you'd like a short one-mile run, follow the signs for the Teign Valley walks. Once you reach the end, turn left over the open common and follow the tramper waymarking. Then you will take the Gorse Blossom Walk, you'll understand how it got its name once there. Once you reach Dolly's Seat, you'll take a right and head down a short, steep slope. Keep on Hunters Path, which will bring you back up to Castle Drogo.

If you'd like a long run around the gorge, you can take the classic circuit. It is 6.6 km long. You'll follow the signs for Teign Valley and then turn right and look for signs for Hunters Path. You should take two flights of steps that will bring you out on the path, turn left, and follow signs for Fingle Bridge. Keep following the trail and the signs for Fingle Bridge. You will reach a spot where you can choose to follow the Fishermans Path, or you can go across the bridge and be brought out at car park. Either route will take you all the way through the gorge.

You can explore the formal gardens as well, but the best running routes are through the gorge.

Chapter 62: Cheddar Gorge, Somerset

This is Britain's largest gorge. It has dramatic cliffs and beautiful stalactite caverns. The cliffs rise more than 450 feet. This is an area that has a lot of natural beauty that shows us many hidden secrets. Some of these secrets are stories from our prehistoric ancestors.

Cheddar Gorge lets you explore Britain's largest gorge. Since it was excavated during the 1890s, Gough's Cave has been given an international reputation because of its geological and historical significance. The "Cheddar Man" was found inside this cave. It is Britain's oldest fully intact skeleton that was discovered in 1903. This is also where you will find the biggest underground river in Britain. If you want to learn more, you can take a guided tour through the caves and visit the Museum of Prehistory.

It doesn't matter if it is sunny or rainy; Cheddar Gorge and Caves will always be a great spot to go exploring.

Chapter 63: Clumber Park, Nottinghamshire

This is an easy trail to discover Clumber's past while enjoying some wildlife on your journey. This is a short walk through history that is great for children. It is an easy trail where you can push your child in a stroller.

Clumber used to be the estate of the Newcastle Dukes. The mansion was destroyed in 1938, the walled garden, lake, pleasure ground, and chapel are still there as clues to its wonderful past. Local conservation and the National Trust take care of all the fauna and flora found on the estate along with its history.

To begin the trail, go to the National Trust parking lot. When you leave the parking lot, you will follow the signs for the restaurant and shop. If you pay close attention, you should see the nests of the housemartin underneath the eaves of the stables. During the late summer, they will be flying about getting ready for their migration in winter. Go through the yew hedge, and you will see where some flagstones mark the outline of the former mansion.

Keep on this path, and it will take you to the chapel. You will need to turn right at the junction right after the chapel. This is the Chapel of St. Mary the Virgin. Its spire is a wonderful backdrop for you to stop and take pictures in front of. It was commissioned in 1886 by Henry Pelham Clinton. He was the seventh Duke of Newcastle. It took the workers three years to get the chapel built. Take the time to look at all the wonderful Victorian ecclesiastical architects that are inside the chapel. There are volunteers on hand to help you find all the stone gargoyles sitting in the window arches and the stained glass. The gargoyles are representative of the seven deadly sins.

Once you leave the chapel and continue on your trail, you will see a mock temple on your left. This was built for the second Duke of Newcastle in 1784. You will notice the contrast between the temple and the one located on the other side of the lake. One is done in a Greek Doric style, and the other one is Roman. Look at all the cedars of Lebanon that stand proud above and enjoy smelling the mock orange shrubbery. If you can be quiet enough, you might just see a mouse scurry by.

Keep following the center path through the gardens. This area located east of the main mansion was built during the 1900s to give the Dukes' families sheltered and secluded walks and seats. It has many wonderful views. You can walk just like they did on the paths that have been restored. The plants located here are normal of the Victorian times as they like collecting exotic trees. Look for hinoki cypress. This was planted in the temple gardens in Japan, where it came from. You should see some rhododendron varieties such as Cunninghams Bush.

You will exit the gardens through a stone gate when the path ends. You will move toward Ash Tree Hill Wook. This is a peculiar name since there isn't one ash tree to be found. You will see on both your right and left the Cow Pasture Field, where many of the flints found during the Bronze Age was found. This shows that people were on this land way before any of the Dukes.

While you are walking through the woods, listen for birds. You should hear drumming coming from all the woodpeckers found here. Look at all the dead timber on this path; you might just find some holes from beetles. When you get to the crossroads, you will need to turn left and follow the track made from red shale.

After you pass the buildings, you will need to take a left when you get to the crossroads and continue along the road and into the Leaping Bar Wood. You will pass The Burrow, which is a soft area to play located to your left.

After you go through the gates in front of you, turn right and go past the chapel. This will take you back to the visitor's center. Since you are there, why don't you grab an afternoon tea or lunch from the café and look through the gift shop and plants for sale?

Chapter 64: Dark Peak, Derbyshire

This is a challenging route that goes through gritstone outcroppings and the Kinder Downfall waterfall that is usually frozen during the winter. To get to the trail, you will need to go from the Bowden Bridge parking lot and follow Kinder Road northeast until you get to Booth Bridge. Next, take the path to White Brow and keep going along the William Clough until you turn right onto Pennine Way. Follow this to Sandy Heys. You will stay on Pennine Way and go past Kinder Downfall and then over the Kinder Low until you come to Edale Cross. You will turn right onto the path there and follow it down the hill until you get back to Hayfield.

This trail has a distance of 14 km or 8.5 miles. You will begin and end at the Bowden Bridge parking lot located on Kinder Road in Hayfield. The track's terrain will be moorland, a slabbed path, and normal trails. This track is a bit challenging, but if you are used to running or hiking, it shouldn't be a problem for you. It has an ascent of 536 meters. If there is good visibility the day you go, you shouldn't have any problems navigating the trails.

Dark Peak is the wilder, higher section in Peak District. It lies mostly in South Yorkshire and Derbyshire. The Millstone Grit makes the landscape look brooding and dark. It is usually wet and peaty. The gritstone outcrops create a type of inverted horseshoe around the lowest part of the White Peak made from limestone. The highest points of Dark Peak include Bleaklow and Kinder Scout.

This is where the High Peak Marathon is done. This is a 4-mile challenge for teams made up of four people. This challenge is made even harder because it is done during the night in March when there is usually ice and snow on the ground. Icy winds will blast along the open moors and drive the rain that brings more misery to the lonely hours before dawn.

During the day and when the weather is nice, running Dark Peak is great. It has miles upon miles of wonderful trails that cover the fells. It can be easily accessed from Sheffield and Manchester. It has train stations and pleasant villages along the course. The Pennine Way starts a 276-mile journey north from Edale and is a challenging run.

This Kinder Trespass was a march of 500 people who were protesting the closure of the moorland to people wanting to run and walk. Access was finally granted in 1932. The run shows the route that the protesters took from the banks of the Kinder River up to the Pennine Way located at Ashop Head. There are plenty of wonderful views that open over the rugged gritstone cliffs and moorland.

Chapter 65: Derwent Water, Cumbria

This trail is 10.8 miles in length. It is near Keswick, Cumbria in England. The trail features a lake is a moderate trail. It gets used for nature trips, running, walking, and hiking.

You probably won't find a better walk in the Lake District that will give you as much as Derwent Water. It is a good distance and gives you a chance to spend an entire day at the lake. This trail goes in a counter-clockwise direction, beginning at the suspension bridge over Derwent River close to Portinscale. There is an option to do Nichol End marina, too, and this is worth the detour.

You will pass through the Linghold Estates woodlands. Your view will get better once you pass the Hawes End Outdoor Center. Once you get to Brandelhow Park, you will see wooden hands that have been carved that celebrate the purchase of the woods. You will then go along Brandelhow Bay and see the house located at Brandelhow Point. Sir Hugh Walpole used to live in the house on the Cat Bells slope. This house is called Brackenburn. During the 1930s, Walpole started writing his historical romance novels known as *Rogue Herries*. These were all set in Cumberland.

You will soon come to Manesty Park and see the boardwalk made from recycled plastic to help you cross over the wettest part of the lake. Please note that this can become covered if there has been a lot of rain in the area. When you cross the bridge that has been renovated, you are halfway through the trail. You can usually see some climbers on Shepherd's Crag most of the time.

You will pass some toilets before you reach the Lodore Hotel. Walkers are welcome to use the toilets if need be. If you can't go any farther, you can take the ferry back to Keswick.

After a short trip through some woodland, you will once again be back on the shore of the lake near the National Trust parking lot. The lake stays fairly low, and walking around it usually isn't a problem, but these conditions can change. If you look at all the debris along the shore, you will be able to see all the different water levels.

When you get to Calfclose Bay, be looking for the centenary stone that is partially submerged. This was placed to celebrate the 100th anniversary of the National Trust. There is a bench where you can sit if you need to. The large island you can see from this point is called Saint Herbert's Island.

Once you pass through the pasture land, the trial will go back inland near Stable Hills, and you will come out at Strandshag Bay. You will see Lord's Island across from this point.

You will follow Frair's Crag. You should see a memorial to Ruskin here. There is a promenade that has just been built, complete with benches and picnic tables at the boat landings. From this point, you can either go through the center of the town of Keswick or cross over to Crow Park from the "Theatre By The Lake." This will take you to the Headlands. Once you have crossed the bridge on the road over the Greta River, you will see a path that runs along the Keswick to the show grounds that will bring you back to the beginning of the trail.

Chapter 66: Lyme, Cheshire

Lyme Park is located in South Disley, Cheshire, England. It is made up of a mansion that is surrounded by formal gardens and a deer park. Sir Thomas Danyers was granted the Estate in 1346, and it was then passed on to the Leghs of Lymes in 1388 by marriage. The Legh family gave it to the National Trust in 1946.

The formal gardens are about 15 acres, and the deer park comes in at just over 1300 acres. The car park is open from 9 AM to 4:30 PM, so be sure you are done before then.

One of the runs you can take is known as "A Walk to the Lantern." It is 2.7 km and is considered a moderate route. Starting in the main car park, you will follow the sloping path at the information center, which will take you towards the house. Keep the house to your right, move along the tarmac road that will take you up a hill on the left. Once past the stables, you will see a gateway on the right. Go through the gate and head towards the next gate that leads you to Turfhouse Meadow. You will then reach a gate and stile. You can climb the stile onto the moor and make your way up the hill following the wall. There will be a deer leap in the wall and then another stile, which you will climb. Then you can move along the path through the woodland. As you wander through the woods, you will eventually find the lantern, which is downhill on the left. You can finish your trek back, continuing along the path, and climb over a stile onto Caters Slack. You'll climb on more stile before taking the road ahead, which will bring you back to the car park.

You can also take the Lyme Park Circular trail. It is a 7.2-mile loop around Lyme Park. It takes you to some of the more unseen corners of the park. If you want to visit the Cage, you can start at the Visitor Centre in Higher Poynton and follow the signs for Haresteads Farms, keeping the woods at your right. You'll go through a wooden gate that takes you into Lyme Park. Once at the front of Lyme Hall, go left, and take the path uphill towards the Cage. Then you can head back down towards the tarmac that runs through Lyme Park.

There are a number of other trails you take in Lyme. Many of these will lead you to historical places that you can enjoy as well.

Chapter 67: Speke Hall, Liverpool

In this race, you will have a chance to have fun and enjoy a beautiful view, peaceful route, and it will give you a wonderful chance to train. If you would like to just do a 5K, you can choose to only run one loop.

Your family and friends can come with you and give you some encouragement and support before and after the race. The restaurant, Speke Hall Home Farm, will be opened early and will serve both cold and hot refreshments. You can have your choice of toast, sausage or bacon sandwiches or tea cakes. These are the perfect refreshment to perk you back up once you have finished the race.

You don't need to register before the race. Just show up the day of the race and be ready. There is only enough space for 200 people so you will need to arrive a bit early to get registered. If you show up too late, you might be turned away. Make sure you take the time before the race begins to fill out emergency contact information, so they have that on hand during the race.

You will register at the Home Farm parking lot. This is where you will sing in at the time given to you. If you do decide to preregister for this race, you need to get there between 8:40 and 8:45. If you don't preregister, you will need to be there between 8:30 and 8:40.

This race can be done by anyone over the age of 14. Children have to be supervised, and they are their guardian or parents' responsibility during the entire race.

You can't take your dog on the race. You are welcome to bring your dog to the park, but they have to be kept on a tight leash and cannot go into any of the formal gardens.

If you are a member of the National Trust, you can bring your ID to scan when you leave. Your membership helps support Speke Hall.

If knowing your time during the race is important to you, you will need to bring a device so you can monitor that on your own.

You will need to be ready and dressed for the race. Make sure to bring some warm clothing and some clean ones that you can change into after the event. Trail shoes or regular running shoes are great for this race. You will not need to add studs to your trail shoes.

If you do decide to run by yourself, get a tag to put your emergency details on in case of an emergency.

Restrooms will open at 8:45 and stay open for the duration of the race.

This route has a mixture of surfaces, gradients, and trails. It goes through coastal reserves and woodlands. You will experience gravel, tarmac, and grass.

Speke Hall will open at 10:30 for visitors. If you want to visit once the race is over, it would be a wonderful addition to your day.

Chapter 68: Cader Idris Mountain Race

This race is considered to be the hardest fell race in Wales. Many runners look at it as a classic and a race they have to do each year.

The race begins and ends in Dolgellau, a market town on sea level. It will climb about 3,000 feet to the top of Pen y Gader. The main challenge of this race is the terrain is always changing. It changes from metalled roads that are very steep to flat trails that run behind Gwernan lake. You will have to go up steps on the Pony Path and then pick your way through the fields of boulders during the last ascent. The fun part is you have to turn around and go back the way you came.

The best way to have success is to try your best not to get leg cramps with the ever-changing road surfaces and the course running from steep to flat. If you manage to finish the course, you will be met with a large cheering crowd.

Chapter 69: Keswick Mountain

The Keswick Mountains lay within the Lake District National Park in Cumbria. It is home to the Keswick Mountain Festival that has been held annually since 2007. Keswick is often the start and endpoint for the Wainwright and Bob Graham Rounds. However, if you aren't a fan of 100-kilometer races, then there are some other Keswick trails that you may enjoy.

If you like something that is shorter, then the Keswick Park Run. This is five laps around the park that will give you a quick five-kilometer run. However, if you don't like the idea of running around in a circle five times, you can do the five-kilometer trail run. It starts at Crow Park before you head through Cockshot Woods until you hit the track alongside Borrowdale Road. Then you head back to Crow Park along the shores of Derwentwater.

If you'd like something longer than a 5K, then you can try the Keswick AC's Skiddaw Fell Race. This covers almost ten miles, but it has a 2700 foot ascent. It starts in Fitz Park. From there, you will travel through Jenkin Hill, Little Man, and Middle top before you hit the summit of Skiddaw. Then you turn and return back to the start along the same route.

If you are an ultra runner, you could try out the Abraham Tea Round. It starts in George Fisher in Keswick and is made up of a 30-mile loop and 12,000+ foot ascent. As you can see, Keswick Mountain is not short on places to run and has something for everybody.

Chapter 70: Isle of Jura

This race is held every May. It begins and ends at Craighouse, which is located on the island of Jura in Scotland. The running course will loop west and then go north over many hills that include the Paps of Jura. Once you have climbed to the top of Corra Bheinn, you will have a boggy descent that will take you to the coastal road that you will follow for the last three miles of the race.

This route is about 27 km or 17 miles longs. It will have an ascent of around 2350 meters. It is known for being a boggy and rocky terrain and extremely hard. Many people like this race because it is so remote and away from a lot of traffic.

Just to get to the start of the race, you will have to take a ferry from Islay and then another ferry to get to Jura. Then you will travel by foot, ride a bicycle for several miles, or take a bus to get to Craighouse.

Most runners will get to the island before the race and stay on the island until the event is over. They will attend the ceilidh that is held with each race each year. They also like catching all the attractions that Jura holds. It was noted that during the 1997 race, that most of the runners were competing for English clubs. Champions Angela Mudge and Ian Holmes have said that Jura is their favorite race.

Because there is such a huge contrast between most of the course's rough terrain and the final few miles of the course, runners have changed from fell shoes to regular running shoes for the last few miles to be able to run better on the tarmac. But some runners experienced cramps from changing shoes.

Conclusion

Once again, thank you for choosing *Great British Running Routes*. I hope you have found the information helpful and informative.

The next step is to visit some of the places and giving these running routes a try. Whether you live near some of these places or you are just visiting, these areas are worth checking out. The important thing is to enjoy the time you spend in these areas.

Finally, I would like to ask that if you found this book helpful, a review would be much appreciated!

Printed in Great Britain
by Amazon

18894545R00058